DEADLY SCIENCE

Animal survival

Contents

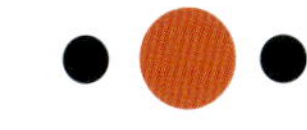

ADJUNCT ASSOCIATE PROFESSOR COREY TUTT OAM

DEADLY SCIENCE

DeadlyScience aims to provide Science, Technology, Engineering and Mathematics (STEM) resources to remote schools around Australia. So far, DeadlyScience has shipped more than 33,000 STEM books and resources to more than 800 schools across the country.

The organisation began when proud Kamilaroi man Corey Tutt found out that some schools in Australia were completely under-resourced and that Aboriginal and Torres Strait Islander children were discouraged from pursuing STEM because of this. DeadlyScience knows from personal experience that books and resources change lives and believes these kids deserve nothing but the best. Aboriginal and Torres Strait Islander peoples in Australia were the First Scientists of this land, and DeadlyScience is committed to preserving that history.

Deadly survival

For all animals, survival is what life is all about. However, survival can be measured in many different ways. A species can be a successful survivor if it has existed for a very long time. It can be seen as a great survivor if it exists where other animals don't, which means it can use resources – food and shelter – that other animals can't. Maybe it has specialist adaptations for surviving in extreme environments, such as the deep ocean or the Australian desert, or even Antarctica. Sometimes, survival is just a matter of luck. In some cases, a species has clung onto life, hidden away in a small part of the world, almost as if it has been forgotten.

PENGUINS

PANDA SNAIL

Occasionally, humans step in to help a species survive, but too often we are the reason it is heading towards extinction in the first place.

LEOPARD SEAL

CORROBOREE FROG

PYGMY-POSSUM

Survivors of time

Extinction is a natural process. Species have been going extinct ever since life first appeared on Earth about 3.7 billion years ago. In fact, most species on Earth – 99.9% of all species that ever evolved – have already gone extinct. This is because habitats and conditions constantly change. Species that can't cope with the changes around them die out and are replaced by new species that can.

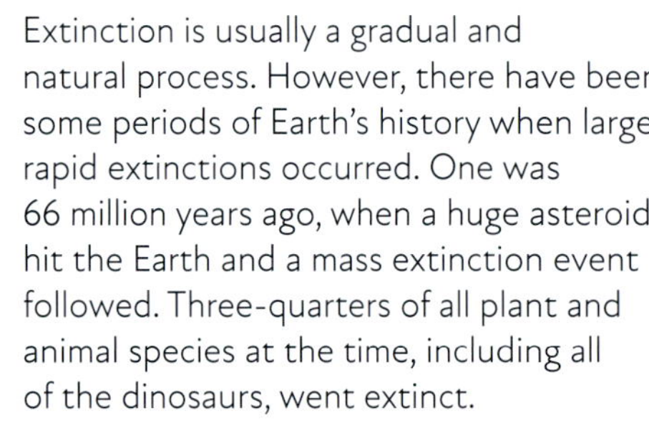

Extinction is usually a gradual and natural process. However, there have been some periods of Earth's history when large, rapid extinctions occurred. One was 66 million years ago, when a huge asteroid hit the Earth and a mass extinction event followed. Three-quarters of all plant and animal species at the time, including all of the dinosaurs, went extinct.

Rate of extinctions

The rate of extinction worldwide is now occurring much faster than would usually be expected. This time, it is mostly caused by human activity, such as habitat destruction, development for cities and agriculture, introduced species, pollution and disease. Known as the Sixth Mass Extinction, this phenomenon is also due to the speed at which the climate is changing on Earth today. But these are topics for another book (or two)! This one is mostly a celebration of survival.

Most species survive 5–10 million years before going extinct. But some species have cheated this statistic to survive much longer. Some sea sponge, jellyfish, and nautilis species, along with horseshoe crabs, have existed for hundreds of millions of years.

Isolation

Australia's animals and plants have been evolving in isolation – separated from the rest of the world – for many millions of years. This is why as much as 80% of our animal life is unique: it doesn't occur anywhere else in the world. This lack of competition from outside Australia has also meant that we have a high proportion of 'living fossils' compared to many other countries. These are species that haven't changed, in some cases, since the age of dinosaurs, or even longer, like the Wollemi pine and king fern.

CHANGING ENVIRONMENTS

Land clearing and the spread of housing developments and agriculture are taking over and altering the natural habitats that animals need to survive.

Queensland lungfish

If you look back far enough, you'll see that all complex life on Earth started out in the ocean. A few species, such as the Queensland lungfish, got stalled while transitioning to land. It has a fully functional lung to breathe air directly – just like a land animal – as well as the gills of a fish, enabling it to absorb oxygen from water. It can survive in disappearing waterholes during long periods of drought.

FACT

It is thought that individual Queensland lungfish can live for up to 100 years. This amazing species has survived on Earth for about 400 million years.

Giant panda snail

The giant panda snail is Australia's largest land snail, reaching a shell length of 9 cm. Even the egg of the giant panda snail is huge, almost the size of a small bird's egg. This snail, which only comes out when it rains, is thought to have been living unchanged for 85 million years in the same place where it first evolved, back when Australia was still attached to Antarctica and India. Back then, Australia was covered in warm, moist forests. Today, you'll find the giant panda snail in southern Queensland and northern New South Wales, where some of these ancient forests still cling to life.

DID YOU KNOW?

Giant panda snails are about the size of a tennis ball.

Velvet worms

These worms were once mistaken for slugs. But they're much more special than that. Velvet worms have survived on Earth for more than 400 million years. They are now known to be so different to any other animals that scientists put them together in their own group – the Onychophora, which means 'claw-bearers'. Most of Australia's velvet worm species are very small – up to 4 cm long – and each has roughly 16 stumpy legs. These strange creatures are mostly found in moist leaf litter and rotting logs on forest floors, and they really do look as if they're made of soft cloth, like velvet.

VELVET WORMS

Australia has the most velvet worm species on Earth – over 74!

But don't be deceived! A velvet worm is a vicious predator that catches small invertebrate prey, such as termites and centipedes, by covering it with a net of sticky slime excreted from glands on its head. Then it eats into its prey's skin and sucks out the nutritious fluids!

LEAF LITTER

STROMATOLITES

DID YOU KNOW?

Stromatolites are the oldest living lifeforms on our planet.

Stromatolites

Until 1961, stromatolites were only known from fossils. But we now know living colonies remain in a few isolated sites in WA and Tasmania. Stromatolites are layered rock-like structures trapped and built up over thousands of years by colonies of microscopic organisms called cyanobacteria. These harness energy from sunlight and produce oxygen in the process. Cyanobacteria were the first known organisms on Earth to photosynthesise and produce oxygen – they're like the earliest plants.

Wollemi pine

This tree species – which was discovered in 1994 in Wollemi National Park, west of Sydney, NSW – is known as "the botanical find of the 20th century". It's thought to have survived 150 million years, and dinosaurs probably munched on its branches. A protective waxy coating that covers growing buds during cold months is thought to have helped the Wollemi pine survive many ice ages. There are fewer than 100 adult trees now known to survive in the wild. Their exact whereabouts are kept secret to protect them.

Did you know?
Wollemi pine trees can grow to 30 m in 100 years.

Dinosaurs may have munched on this ancient tree's branches!

FACT
Crocodiles have a pointed snout, while alligators have a rounded one.

On Badu Island, the name for a crocodile is koedal. It is a totem animal for some families too.

Saltwater crocodile

If this northern Australian species wasn't around when dinosaurs ruled the Earth, then species very similar to it were. It's superbly well adapted to its environment and is thought to have remained virtually unchanged for more than 50 million years. The saltwater crocodile is the largest living reptile species on Earth: males grow to a length of 6 m and a weight of 1000 kg.

Indigenous people used hand-carved spears to hunt crocodiles for meat.

Food source

Crocodiles are extremely important to First Nations cultures in northern Australia, and some Aboriginal and Torres Strait Islander peoples have the crocodile as their totem. Although larger crocodiles are respectfully left alone, smaller crocodiles are often caught and eaten. Crocodile eggs are also regarded as a particularly nutritious food source.

SPEAR TIPS

The Gamilaraay word for an echidna is bigibila. It is also a food item in some communities.

Short-beaked echidna

This species of termite-eating, egg-laying mammal is only found in Australia, although it has close relatives in Papua New Guinea. So far, the oldest-known fossil echidna has been dated to 17 million years ago and was found in a cave in eastern Australia, but the species is thought to be much older. It lives in a wide range of habitats, from alpine areas to the edges of deserts.

DID YOU KNOW?

The short-beaked echidna has one of the widest distributions of any native Australian mammal.

Mountain shrimp

This freshwater shrimp species lives only in Tasmania but is related to shrimps found in South America and New Zealand. This suggests it must have evolved before Australia split away from those landmasses about 180 million years ago. Fossils found in lake sediments in NSW are identical to this Tasmanian species and are 220 million years old.

FACT

Mountain shrimp are adapted to very tough habitats in high-country, cold-water Tasmanian streams and caves.

Photograph: John Gooderham @ Tasmanian Threatened Species. **Photograph:** Simon Grove @ Tasmanian Museum.

DID YOU KNOW?

The male platypus has a spur on its back feet to inject a powerful venom!

The Wurundjeri name for platypus is dulaiwarrung.

Platypus

When British museum curators in the 18th century first saw a platypus skin, which was sent from Australia, they thought it was a hoax created by stitching parts of other animals together. The platypus is grouped, along with echidnas, into a separate order of mammals called monotremes. Like reptiles, monotremes lay eggs, but like other mammals, they nurture their young on milk, which suggests they are a missing link between these two groups. Scientists know that platypus-like animals were once more widespread because the oldest platypus fossils come from 61-million-year-old rocks in South America.

FACT

According to a First Nations legend, a female duck mated with a lonely water rat to make the first platypus.

Survivors of cold

Kunama is the word for snow in the Ngarigo language.

Despite having vast areas of hot, arid landscapes, Australia also has some cold – even alpine – places, both on the mainland and in Tasmania. Plenty of animal species there are specially adapted to surviving freezing conditions. Australia also has a few of the coldest places on Earth in some of its offshore territories, notably on Antarctic islands and the Antarctic mainland. Some of the world's best survivors of extreme cold live there.

Corroboree frogs

Australia's two species of corroboree frog are both found in a very small subalpine area of Kosciusko National Park, NSW. Sadly, both are critically endangered due to a fungal disease and habitat destruction. They have the same sort of life cycle as most other frogs: tadpoles hatch from eggs and live in water until they change into adults, when they live on land. However, in corroboree frogs, the eggs develop at first but stop growing for a while and enter a period of suspended growth known as a 'diapause'. They start developing again and then hatch after rainfall or melted snow in late winter has flooded their nest. By accumulating poisons in their skin from the ants they eat, corroboree frogs are protected from most predators. Their bright colouration is an indicator that they are poisonous and warns would-be predators to stay away.

Corroboree

Corroboree is a general term coined by early British settlers in Sydney. They adapted it from the local Dharug word garaabara and used it to describe First Nations dance and music ceremonies, which often involved costumes and body decoration. Corroboree frogs were given their common name because their bold stripes mirror the paint people often adorned their bodies with during these ceremonies. Some First Nations Australians use the term corroboree, but there are also many other words in local languages for celebratory events.

CORROBOREE FROG

BOGONG MOTH

This moth's name comes from the word bugung (brown) of the Dhudhuroa Nation.

FLYING FOOD

Bogong moths, which arrive in their billions, represent a huge influx of high-fat, high-protein insect food and are critical to the alpine ecosystem.

Bogong moth

Millions of adult bogong moths spend summers resting in a dormant state, living off their fat reserves and sheltering in rock crevices in the Australian Alps. As winter approaches and temperatures fall, they take off in a huge mass migration, heading for breeding grounds in Queensland and NSW. In summer, they fly back the other way, returning to the mountains. They've been doing the same thing and following the same migration routes for many thousands of years.

MOUNTAIN PYGMY-POSSUM

Mountain pygmy-possum

The mountain pygmy-possum is the only Australian mammal that lives permanently in an alpine region. It can do this because it fattens itself up for a winter hibernation by gorging in summer on bogong moths. In winter, it curls up in a ball under an insulating layer of snow and hibernates through the coldest months of the year. This possum was thought to be extinct before it was rediscovered in the 1960s.

Seal with spots

A thick layer of fat known as blubber helps to keep leopard seals warm in the freezing waters of Antarctica, where they hunt for penguins. Being so large also helps mammals such as these seals stay warmer in cold conditions because they have more muscle to generate heat and less body area to lose it from. These predatory seals can survive in subzero sea temperatures. Female leopard seals, which are larger than males, can weigh up to 500 kg. The only predators of these large carnivorous seals are orcas (killer whales).

Emperor penguin

Adult emperor penguins have multiple layers of scale-like feathers to keep out freezing blizzards in Antarctica, where they breed. Adults with chicks and eggs will huddle together to stay warm, an important behaviour to help survive the cold. Special fats in their feet stop them from freezing on the ice. These birds also have lots of overall body fat to provide them with energy and insulation. Another adaptation is that they can 'recycle' their own body heat. This is done by blood flowing away from the heart in arteries, passing close to veins travelling in the other direction. This means that blood is pre-cooled as it heads towards the penguin's feet, wings and bill but warmed on its way back before reaching the heart.

FACT

Unlike most other species of seal, leopard seals prefer a solitary life. They don't form colonies and like to hunt alone. The only time they seek company is when they are breeding.

DID YOU KNOW?

Female emperor penguins lay a single egg each year and leave it with their mate while they go out to sea to hunt and feed for nine weeks. The male balances the egg on his feet to keep it off the snow until it hatches.

DID YOU KNOW?

Antarctica is the only continent that has no native terrestrial (land) mammals, only marine wildlife and birds.

Icefishes

Icefishes are specially adapted to surviving in the bitterly cold waters of the Southern Ocean around Antarctica. They have a special protein in their blood that acts like an antifreeze to stop their blood from freezing in the icy conditions.

PENGUIN

Desert survivors

Much of Australia is hot and dry. In fact, after Antarctica, Australia is the driest continent in the world. About one-third of the Australian mainland receives so little rain it could be classified as desert, and three-quarters is so dry that it is classified as arid or semi-arid. And yet, there are plenty of animal species surviving in these places. You just might need to look hard for them.

Southern marsupial mole

This endangered desert dweller lives almost exclusively underground and is a superb burrower that 'swims', rather than digs, through sand. It leads with its calloused nose and forehead, followed by its spade-shaped feet and well-developed shoulders. Because marsupial moles need very little oxygen, they can survive by breathing in air trapped between sand grains. And because they don't need to see, as they live their entire life almost completely underground, marsupial moles are blind – they have eyes, but they don't function at all.

SOUTHERN MARSUPIAL MOLE

The southern marsupial mole is called itjaritjari in several First Nations languages.

Its Pitjantjatjara/ Yankunytjatjara name is tarkawara.

SPINIFEX HOPPING-MOUSE

Spinifex hopping mouse

Like many desert mammals, this little native Australian rodent avoids the daytime heat and only comes out at night to forage for food. It has the most efficient kidneys of any mammal in the world, which means this rodent can remove every last drop of water from its urine, making it almost solid. Because of this, the spinifex hopping mouse can survive for long periods without drinking water.

FACT

While this spinifex looks inhospitable, it is a lifesaver to species looking for water.

Red kangaroo

This roo is the biggest Australian marsupial. Males, which are much larger than the females, grow to more than 1.8 m in height. Using their strong hind legs, the red kangaroo can cover almost 8 m in a single leap and bound across desert sands at speeds of almost 60 kmph. It's a great way to travel to distant food patches surviving in arid areas. One of their many adaptations to desert survival is on their forearms: there they have a dense network of blood vessels near the skin's surface. Red kangaroos lick this area and, through a process called evaporative cooling, heat from inside the body is released and blows away in the desert wind. Red kangaroos are also inactive during the hottest part of the day.

RED KANGAROO

The Gamilaraay name for kangaroo is bawurra.

TRUE SURVIVORS

First Nations peoples have looked for clues in nature to survive for tens of thousands of years in some of the planet's most arid environments.

Thorny devil

The thorny devil comes out by day to feed on small insects. Its body colouration makes it hard for its main predators, birds of prey, to see it against desert sands. The spikes all over its body are for defence and are also a clever way of catching dew drops, which the devil collects each morning by rubbing up against spinifex. Through a process known as capillary action, the tiny droplets of water run down the grooves between the spikes and straight into the devil's mouth.

THORNY DEVIL

The Arrernte name for a thorny devil is unyerre.

Camel

Almost every aspect of a camel's physiology is adapted to life in the desert. Most noticeably, camels respond to hot, arid conditions by reducing urine production, concentrating their urine, and sweating economically. Camels are not native to Australia. They were brought here by Europeans in the 1800s, mainly for use as outback transport. However, they are so superbly adapted to the desert environment that their numbers have continued to grow. Now, Central Australia has one of the world's largest populations of dromedary camels – at about one million camels.

The Pitjantjatjara word for bilby is ninu.

GREATER BILBY

Greater bilby

Bilbies use their strong front limbs to dig deep, corkscrew-shaped, underground burrows, where they shelter from the desert sun. Their huge, near-naked ears help release body heat but also provide bilbies with very good hearing to find insect prey at night. While bilbies have outstanding senses of smell and hearing, they have extremely poor eyesight.

CAMEL

Water-holding frogs can survive for years underground in arid areas. During desert rains, they take in large amounts of water before surface moisture evaporates.

FACT

In the deserts, water-holding frogs can be a vital water source for First Nations people.

Crucifix frog

This burrowing, arid-zone frog can live in a type of suspended animation up to 3 m underground for years at a time, waiting for rain. At the first few drops, it digs its way to the surface – like most desert-dwelling frogs – to feed and breed like crazy before heading back underground to wait for the next shower. It keeps moist while underground by secreting a protective cocoon around itself. The bright colours of the crucifix frog are a warning sign to potential predators that it is poisonous to eat.

CRUCIFIX FROG

The Rainbow Serpent

The creation stories of First Nations people document their history, cultures and beliefs. They also speak of the environments where people live or come from and the natural elements that are found there, including the animals, plants and landforms.

Throughout the hundreds of different First Nations cultures in Australia, there are certainly some similarities and recurring themes in these accounts. But each language group also has its own distinct creation stories, which have been passed down from generation to generation for more than 60,000 years.

Science and historical events are often blended in these stories. They tell of how life and the landscape came to be and offer important lessons for survival in the harsh Australian environment. Many events these stories describe match scientific understanding of ancient geological events. Some stories, for example, describe significant landscape changes, such as the sea level rise that occurred 7000 years ago after the last ice age, or asteroid strikes. Other stories recall now-extinct animals.

The Rainbow Serpent is a mythical creature that is known by many names and appears in various forms in First Nations creation stories. It is often involved in the creation of local landscapes and waterways. This important Dreamtime reptile tends to live in permanent waterholes and controls water, which, of course, is fundamental to all life.

WOLFE CREEK CRATER
In the Djaru language, this crater is known as Kandimalal.

LEGEND

The Djaru people consider the Wolfe Creek crater, WA, to be the spot where the rainbow serpent crashed into Earth.

The origins of the Rainbow Serpent are thought to stem from the fact that most snakes, even in the desert, are found close to permanent water. Southern Queensland's Bidjara people know this being as Mundagudda, a serpent that began a journey in Central Queensland's Carnarvon Ranges and travelled through the landscape, creating rivers and gorges. It is because of stories such as this that the starting places of many rivers are known.

First Nations artwork of a Dreamtime serpent is found at Betoota, south-west of Longreach in Queensland on Mithaka Country.

Deep-ocean survivors

Just like it is the world over, the deep sea off Australia is our least-explored habitat. It's a place where there's a lack of light and food, and it's mostly very cold. Importantly, the immense weight of water pressing down from above means the oceans are places where animals are exposed to enormous pressure. Being on the bottom of the deep ocean can be like having a jumbo jet sitting on top of you! To visit the deep, an animal has to have some very special adaptations. To live there permanently, it needs even more extreme and specialised skills.

Southern elephant seal

Elephant seals can dive to 2 km below the surface. No other seal can do that. A range of special adaptations to create and conserve energy in their bodies allows them to make these massive dives. First, this seal's shape underwater looks like a torpedo, which means it can glide through the water effortlessly. Second, a range of special features in elephant seal blood that allow it to take a breath and make the oxygen last for hours.

SOUTHERN ELEPHANT SEAL

Sea pigs

Of course there aren't pigs living in the deep oceans! Sea pigs are actually sea cucumbers – a group of animals related to sea urchins and starfish. They're plump little creatures with as many as seven pairs of 'legs', which they use to trundle across the sea floor, grazing the bottoms of the oceans as far down as 6 km. Sea pigs have mouths ringed by feeding tentacles that they use to vacuum up bits of debris from the sea floor, such as tiny pieces of rotting whale carcass that float down from above.

SEA PIGS

Not all sea cucumbers live in deep-ocean environments. Relatives of sea pigs are plentiful in shallow tropical waters of Australia, and First Nations people in coastal Arnhem Land communities have been harvesting them for centuries. As rock art that dates back to the early 1700s shows, the people of Arnhem Land developed a lasting relationship with Indonesian fishermen who arrived looking for sea cucumbers, known as trepang. This was Australia's first international trading system, and the words used in Arnhem Land for canoe and knife come from Indonesian languages.

Blobfish

The blobfish lives about 1000 m down in waters off Australia and New Zealand. The surrounding pressure at that depth is 120 times what it is on the surface and would crush a body with bones. The blobfish's answer? Have no bones. Its soft body mass is instead supported by the surrounding pressure. The blobfish literally floats in the water just above the ocean bottom, waiting to make a meal out of passing crustaceans or molluscs. In its own deep-sea environment, it would look a lot more like a normal fish, not the blobby mess it collapses into when it is brought to the surface by deep-sea trawlers!

The blobfish has few muscles, so it doesn't move much. It floats just above the sea floor, vacuuming up microscopic food particles.

BLOBFISH

Photographs: Kerryn Parkinson/Australian Museum; Dean Sewell.

Cuvier's beaked whale

One of the few times anyone sees a Cuvier's beaked whale is when the species strands on beaches along the coastlines of Australia and New Zealand, which they do quite often. This whale, which grows to about 7 m long and 3 t in weight, has been recorded diving to almost 3 km deep and staying underwater for more than three hours at a time. That's deeper and longer than any other whale species. Whales breathe air, so exactly how they can spend so much time underwater so deep and for so long is yet to be understood. They do, however, have one amazing adaptation we know of that helps them dive so deeply. They have pocket-like folds on the sides of their bodies, where they can tuck away their flippers to make them more streamlined so they can glide through the water. It's also thought that they may be able to collapse their rib cage and lungs to cope with the extreme pressure of the deep sea.

CUVIER'S BEAKED WHALE

Cuvier's beaked whales feed mostly on squids and octopuses.

Did you know? The orange roughy can live to 100!

ORANGE ROUGHY

Orange roughy

Scientists used to call these deep-sea fish slimeheads. The common name was changed when people began catching them to eat and the name slimehead didn't make it sound appealing. This predatory fish that grows to about 76 cm in length is now known as the orange roughy due to its colour. You'd think orange would make it stand out to the prey it is trying to catch. But at the depths where it lives – 700 to 1400 m below the ocean's surface off south-eastern Australia – there's either no light or very little red light, so being orange makes it seem almost invisible.

FACT

The zombie worms that drill into bones are all females. The males are microscopic and live inside the bodies of the females.

Zombie worms

These deep-sea worms are often found in the decaying remains of whales on the ocean floor. They burrow deep into the bones of these animal corpses to reach the nutritious substance within and feed on that. But they have no functioning mouth, stomach or anus, so they use bacteria living inside them to digest their grisly meals for them.

Coffinfish

The mysterious little deep-sea coffinfish has blue eyes and red feet-like fins, and it belongs to the anglerfish group. It lives up to 2 km deep off Australia, and it attracts unsuspecting prey by using a lure on top of its head that looks like a fishing rod tipped with a fluffy bait.

The coffinfish has specially adapted fins that allow it to 'walk' on the floor of the ocean.

City survivors

Natural habitats provide animals with places to shelter and food to eat, so the habitat destruction that comes with urban sprawl is impossible for some to handle. To avoid humans, many animals move away, or their numbers dwindle. Sadly, some even become extinct. But some species are more resilient than others. For quite a few species in Australia – those that aren't fussy about what they eat or where they sleep – living around people has boosted their survival.

Silver gull

Yes, this aggressive scavenger flocks around us at the beach, begging for our hot chips. There weren't always so many silver gulls in Australia. However, they do very well surviving in our cities, living off our food scraps, so their numbers have exploded since the middle of last century. They breed with other seabirds at colonies on islands off Australia's coasts. But there are now so many silver gulls at these sites that they force out other seabirds such as terns.

Eastern banjo frog

Frogs often don't survive well in urban areas. But the banjo frog is one that has. Five subspecies survive in cities and suburbs right across eastern Australia, including Tasmania. They like to live near water and backyard ponds, so waterways near city parks suit them well.

FACT

The common name for this cheeky bird came from the Yuwaalaraay First Nations people of north-west New South Wales. In early European records, it was first written as galar, gillar and gulah.

Galah

The spread of agriculture across Australia has seen numbers of this pink-and-grey parrot boom since Europeans first arrived over 230 years ago. They're seed eaters that have adapted well to eating grain crops grown by humans, such as wheat and barley. The species used to be restricted to much of inland Australia, but it is now found throughout Australia, including in coastal areas. Galahs are even in Tasmania now but are not native to the area.

PEREGRINE FALCON

Peregrine falcon

Peregrine falcons are the fastest animals in the world, able to swoop on prey at speeds of up to 300 km/h. They live all over the world and have adapted well to life in big cities, including those in Australia. They particularly like tall buildings, which give these raptors a high vantage point from which to watch for prey. They will even make their nests on the window ledges of skyscrapers. These falcons also like to eat introduced rats and mice, so you'll sometimes see peregrine falcons soaring above our cities looking for rodent prey. In this way, falcons perform a helpful pest-control role.

Rainbow lorikeet

One of the most commonly sighted birds in Australia, rainbow lorikeets are loud and vibrant, which makes them hard to miss. But there's also huge flocks of them around our cities. This species is now found way beyond where it originally occurred, which was in eastern and northern Australia. These days, they range even as far west as Perth – thousands of kilometres outside of their natural range. Rainbow lorikeets have been seen taking over nesting hollows of local bird species in Perth, dragging their nestlings out and dropping them on the ground.

RAINBOW LORIKEET

BRUSHTAIL POSSUM
The Wiradjuri word for possum is wilay.

Brushtail possum

Brushtail possums occur in a range of natural habitats, from rainforest and arid-zone woodlands to eucalypt forests. A highly adaptable mammal, they survive well in disturbed landscapes in and around Australia's cities and towns, where they're found in parks and backyards that have lots of trees. Brushtail possums have even been known to move into and live in the roofs of people's homes. Brushtails were introduced to New Zealand in the mid-1800s to support a fur industry, but they adjusted to life there so well that their population grew and the species spread right across the country. In fact, their numbers have grown so much in New Zealand that the species is now one of the country's worst feral pests.

Eastern brown snake

The natural habitat of the eastern brown snake, which can grow up to 2.4 m long, includes woodlands and grasslands. But it copes well with human activity, thrives in cleared areas, and loves to eat introduced mice and rats. Because of that, it's now one of Australia's most commonly encountered snakes. That's unfortunate, as brown snake venom is very potent. This, coupled with their wide distribution, sees brown snakes being responsible for more human deaths in Australia than any other snake species. That title used to belong to the tiger snake, which hasn't coped so well with urban sprawl.

EASTERN BROWN SNAKE
The Eora and Dharug peoples call this snake marragawan.

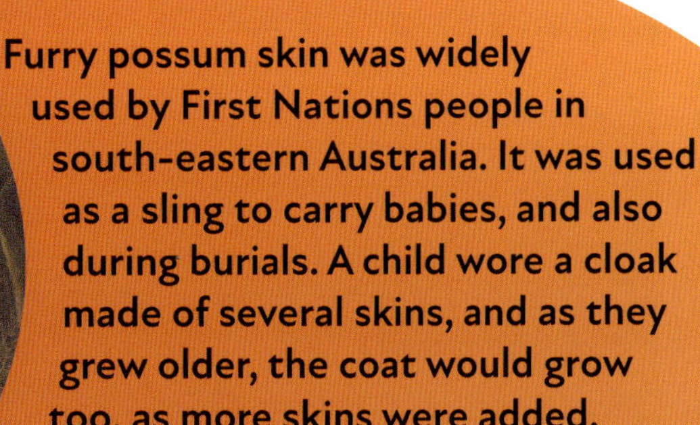

POSSUM-SKIN CLOAKS

Furry possum skin was widely used by First Nations people in south-eastern Australia. It was used as a sling to carry babies, and also during burials. A child wore a cloak made of several skins, and as they grew older, the coat would grow too, as more skins were added.

Extinction survivors

NIGHT PARROT

As has already been mentioned, extinction is a natural part of life on Earth. Most animal species that exist will eventually go extinct. But Australia, like the rest of the world, is facing an extinction crisis and losing species at an unnatural rate – faster than ever before. Our interference with the natural world through things such as clearing forests, pollution and climate change are forcing many animal species to the brink of existence. But occasionally, a species we thought we'd lost forever is found clinging to life.

Fact

According to University of Queensland night parrot researcher Nick Leseberg, who worked with Ngururrpa and Kiwirrkurra rangers to record night parrot calls over six months, there may be 50–60 birds surviving in the 100 km of land that was surveyed.

Night parrot

This very rare species of parrot lives on the ground, is active at night, and is threatened by feral cats. During the 1800s, it had been reported in arid and semi-arid areas in all mainland states. But from the early 1900s, after no confirmed records of it for almost 80 years, it was presumed to be extinct – until it was rediscovered in 2013 in western Queensland! Since then, at least two more tiny populations have been found in Western Australia. The species is now classified as endangered.

LORD HOWE ISLAND STICK INSECT

Lord Howe Island stick insect

Also known as a tree lobster, this very large insect was thought to have been hunted to extinction last century by black rats, which had been introduced to its Lord Howe Island home. In 2001, climbers discovered a small number on a tiny volcanic outcrop called Balls Pyramid, located in treacherous ocean waters about 20 km off Lord Howe Island. Balls Pyramid is so hard to access that it took another two years for rangers to plan the rescue mission to recover some of the surviving stick insects. Two breeding pairs were recovered in 2003 and have since been used to build up numbers of the species. This unusual stick insect is now classified as critically endangered.

Melbourne Zoo is working hard on a breeding program to help this very special insect.

Photograph: Dr Steve Murphy.

DID YOU KNOW?

Turtles are a big part of First Nations culture, as both a totem and as part of Dreaming stories.

Western swamp tortoise

Australia's rarest reptile is the western swamp tortoise. It was thought to have been extinct for more than 100 years until it was rediscovered by a schoolboy in 1953. It was found clinging to survival in a small area of natural habitat that foxes hadn't yet reached. Its main threats are habitat destruction and predation by introduced predators, particularly foxes and feral pigs. There are two wild populations of this turtle, both near Perth. Another two populations have been established about 80 km further north, and captive breeding is building up its numbers. It is, however, still critically endangered.

WESTERN SWAMP TORTOISE

The Noongar word for the western swamp tortoise is yarkiny.

The big picture

Everyone should know by now that the planet – and that includes Australia – is facing an extinction crisis. Many of our species are in trouble. In Australia, we've already lost just over 10% – that's 33 – of the 320 mammal species that lived on this land when Europeans arrived little more than two centuries ago.

It's already too late for the Tasmanian tiger. No one has seen one of those since the 1930s. It's already too late for the paradise parrot, which was reportedly stunning but hasn't been seen since 1926. No one is ever likely to see the desert bandicoot again: it was last seen before 1960. And we haven't seen the bizarre gastric-brooding frogs since the mid-1980s. There were two species, and in both the mother swallowed her eggs, raised tadpoles in her stomach, and fully formed live baby frogs emerged from her mouth (seriously!).

You shouldn't need any other reason than 'because' to want to stop extinctions like these and keep such strange and beautiful creatures alive on the Earth. But another good reason is that if animal and plant species are rapidly disappearing from the planet, we're likely to follow!

So, even if you don't see the beauty in a stunningly coloured Gouldian finch (one of the world's most beautiful birds, which is endangered and found only in northern Australia), and even if you don't marvel at the extraordinary sight of a red kangaroo (see page 17) loping across the Red Centre at 60 km/h in 8 m-long bounds, and even if you aren't awestruck by a tree species like the Wollemi pine that's been around since the dinosaurs (see page 8), then surely you want us humans to survive and to do it in a world with clean air and water and plenty to eat, because saving these species and others means saving yourself, too.

GASTRIC-BROODING FROG

It's estimated that fewer than 2500 mature Gouldian finches exist in the wild.

GOULDIAN FINCH

How do we do that?

Parks, reserves, sanctuaries and similar havens are probably the best answer. A lot of research shows that when you protect a parcel of land and keep everything in it intact, which is what these places aim to do, you don't just save one species, you can save a whole ecosystem: the plants an animal lives on, the animal itself, and the animals that eat it.

This strategy is not all about locking away tracts of land. It's about keeping land safe for the plants and animals that survive there, so people can walk through its woodlands or forests, climb its mountains, or swim in its rivers and enjoy the wildlife that is there – kind of like a big, open-air zoo without bars and cages.

Photographs: Shutterstock, Martin Willis for AWC, and Queensland Museum.

World Heritage Areas

World Heritage Areas (WHAs) are places that Australia should save for the good of the Earth and everything on it. Australia has at least 20 WHAs, many of which are designed to help conserve plants, animals, ecosystems and culture. They include Uluṟu–Kata Tjuṯa, the Great Barrier Reef, Shark Bay, K'gari/Fraser Island, Lord Howe Island, and Kakadu.

Indigenous Protected Areas

First Nations Australians kept their Country healthy for the 60,000 or more years they were its sole custodians, taking care of the animals and plants and using them wisely and sustainably.

Today, a large part of Australia's National Reserve System is made up of Indigenous Protected Areas (IPAs), where First Nations Australians continue to do the job of protecting the Country, as they have done for millennia.

At least 81 dedicated IPAs exist, covering more than 85 million hectares – that's more than 49% of this continent's National Reserve System. Most of these IPAs are managed by Indigenous ranger groups who are dedicated to balancing conservation with other sustainable use, including cultural, social and economic benefits for local First Nations communities.

These places are critically important to the survival of Australia's biodiversity, so land managers combine the best of traditional and contemporary conservation knowledge to achieve the best outcomes for the plants, animals and people who live there together.

Survival stakes

Badu Campus dioramas

People encounter animal habitats each and every day; however, we don't always notice. If we want to help them, we have to pay attention. Simple things such as not cutting down trees, planting native plants and leaving out water can save animals. Badu Campus students thought about that when they produced these great dioramas. In order to understand how animals can survive and thrive in the Torres Strait, they used cultural insight and local knowledge to examine animal movements with the seasons and learn more about animal adaptations.

KINGSTON

FRANK

What to do

1. Choose the animals to focus on for your diorama.
2. Draw and label a picture of your plan. List and label the resources you will use.
3. Find an old box to re-use for the diorama and create the background for your animal, e.g. sky, sea or land.
4. Add elements by using different materials that support your animal's survival, i.e. food and shelter.
5. Label key aspects of the diorama, either using traditional language or English (or both).
6. Share your key information on animal survival with your classmates.

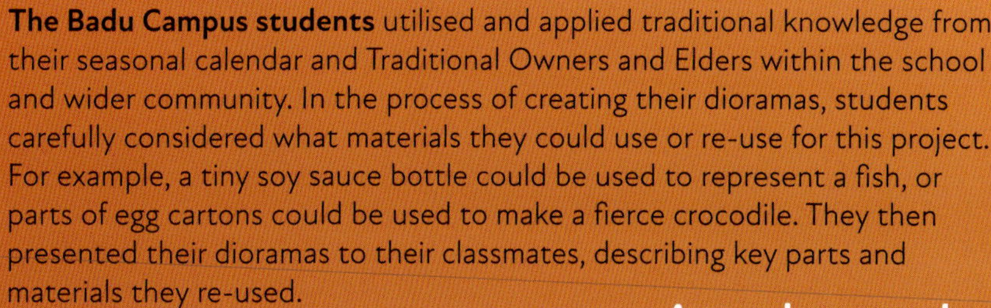

The Badu Campus students utilised and applied traditional knowledge from their seasonal calendar and Traditional Owners and Elders within the school and wider community. In the process of creating their dioramas, students carefully considered what materials they could use or re-use for this project. For example, a tiny soy sauce bottle could be used to represent a fish, or parts of egg cartons could be used to make a fierce crocodile. They then presented their dioramas to their classmates, describing key parts and materials they re-used.

Animal survival

Hardie Grant acknowledges the Traditional Owners of the Country on which we work, the Wurundjeri People of the Kulin Nation and the Gadigal People of the Eora Nation, and recognises their continuing connection to the land, waters and culture. We pay our respects to their Elders past and present.

Hardie Grant Children's Publishing
Wurundjeri Country
Level 11, 36 Wellington Street
Collingwood Victoria 3066
Melbourne | Sydney | San Francisco
hardiegrant.com/childrens
www.australiangeographic.com.au
ISBN: 9781761217999
First published 2021
This edition published 2026

Series editor Corey Tutt **Illustrator** Mim Cole / Mimmim
Designer Harmony Southern

Publisher Penelope White **Editor** Savannah Hollis
Cover design Andy Warren **Internal design** Hannah Janzen
Production Sally Davis

Printed in China by LEO Paper Products LTD

The paper this book is printed on is from FSC® certified forests and other controlled sources. FSC® promotes environmentally responsible, socially beneficial and economically viable management of the world's forests.

10 9 8 7 6 5 4 3 2 1

A catalogue record for this book is available from the National Library of Australia

Picture credits

Front Cover: BMJ/Shutterstock (SS); Ken Griffiths/SS; Kima/SS; Chones/SS; Peter J. Wilson/SS; Benson HE/SS; **2–3:** slowmotiongli/SS; **3:** Ken Griffiths/SS; Alexey Seafarer/SS; Ken Griffiths/SS. **4:** Potapovaladin/SS; Hein Nouwens/SS; Snowshill/SS; **5:** Neupokoev/SS; **6:** paparazzza/SS; Rodica Vasiliev/SS; NinaM/SS; Kapustin Igor/SS; **7:** skippy666/SS; Brian Magnier/Dreamstime; Neil Stanners/SS; PomInPerth/SS; **8:** Carole MacDonald/SS; Herschel Hoffmeyer/SS; **9:** dioch/SS; defpicture/SS; ChameleonsEye/SS. **10:** Jukka Jantunen/SS; John Gooderham/Tasmanian Threatened Species; **11:** worldswildlifewonders/SS; Slowmotiongli/CanvaPro; Florence-Joseph McGinn/SS; Ken Griffiths/SS. **12:** Greg Brave/SS; **13:** ChameleonsEye/SS; Kevin Stead/AG; Ross Dunstan/AG; Ego Guiotto/SS. **14:** Szakharov/SS. **14–15:** vladsilver/SS. **15:** Feathercollector/SS. **16:** idiz/SS; Auscape International Pty Ltd/Alamy; **17:** Ken Griffiths/SS; DianN2/SS; Bradley Blackburn/SS; Janelle Lugge/SS; **18:** Ken Griffiths/SS; konradrza/SS; **19:** Matt Deakin/SS; KajaNi/SS; **20:** fieldwork/SS; Jeremy Richards/SS; **21:** e2dan/SS; Dean Sewell/Australian Geographic (AG); **22:** Andreas Izzotti/SS; Mark Yokoyama/SS; **23:** The Natural History Museum/Alamy; Kelvin Aitken/VWPics/Alamy; **24:** Sasimoto/SS; Peta Buckley Photography/SS; Angata/SS; **25:** Ken Griffiths/SS; On the Wing Photography/SS; Samantha Hopley/SS; **26:** Steve Murphy/AG; Zoos Victoria; Steve Todd/SS; **27:** john austin/SS; **28:** Hein Nouwens/SS; Queensland Museum; Martin Willis/AMC; **29:** Sebastien Burel/SS; MintImages/SS; Francesco Scatena/SS; **30–31:** Deadly Science.

Support trusted, independent, Australian-owned media with a focus on celebrating Australia through compelling stories of its people, places, and natural environment.

Australian Geographic contributes 100% of its profits to the Australian Geographic Society, including its conservation and sustainability programs.

We seek to inspire Australians to love and care for our country and, through the support of the Australian Geographic Society, to empower individuals and organisations to tackle environmental challenges and find innovative solutions to the many threats faced by our natural world.

AUSTRALIAN GEOGRAPHIC SOCIETY
Enquiries about sponsorship and donations:
02 9136 7206
Email: society@ausgeo.com.au
www.australiangeographic.com.au/society

AUSTRALIAN GEOGRAPHIC SUBSCRIPTIONS
Sales and customer enquiries: 1300 555 176
australiangeographic.com.au/product-category/subscriptions